UNDER THE LADDER TO HEAVEN

Poems

by Julia Stein

1984 West End Press

Acknowledgements are made to the following publications in which some of these poems first appeared: *Obras*, *Alcatraz 3*, *Electrum* and the *Unrealist*.

for my mother and father

ISBN 0-931122-36-8

West End Press
Box 7232
Minneapolis, MN 55407

TABLE OF CONTENTS

LILITH

for Doris Lemieux

I. LILITH AND THE ANGEL IN THE DESERT

The angel flew straight at me,
landed with a thick thud,
blared like a winged buffoon,
"The Lorrrddd Goooddd Kinnnggg of the"
I stood up, screamed,
"The Lord made us at the same time,
Lilith and Adam,
out of the same earth.
Paradise was ours. TOGETHER.
Then Adam ordered me
to lie under him when making love.
Orders!
I cut out,
I split,
I flew away."
His wings folded up,
"Adam wants you back."
"No. Never."
"Lilith, if you don't go back
you will be an outcast.
Forever.
We will spread tales about you.
Men will hate you
Women will fear you."
"Get lost, Angel."
"If you don't go back to Adam
you will birth demons."
"Better demons."

II. LILITH GROWS A GARDEN

I give birth to angels
out of my ears, my nose, my mouth.
My children find me
seeds, sprouts, twigs,
search for water,
help me grow a garden,
here in the desert.
I've heard stories from them.
Adam got himself a new wife. Eve.
Docile. Sweet. Does his bidding.
My children bring me the lies
God and Adam tell about me.
At night in his sleep Adam's penis
grows erect, wanting me.
He blames it all on me.
He would.
More lies: I steal their children.
Why should I?
I have thousands of my own.
Why should I ever go back there
when my garden is blooming.
In my garden
all the plants, the animals
grow in freedom.
Not like Eden
where Adam is the boss.
Years ago a girl came, the first.
She said she was unhappy back there,
heard the tales about me and set off.
I let her stay.
More girls came. A boy.
I let them all stay.
I see more come.
Three this time.
Welcome to my garden.
I am Lilith.

GITL

Blessed is Gitl,
great-grandmother from the shtetl,
with your endless prayers,
morning, afternoon, and evening,
even the names you gave your children were prayers,
the first son, Chaim, life,
the first daughter, Esther, saviour,

with your whole life-for-the-children,
the queen of stretching food,
take six potatoes, make a meal for nine,
take one herring, divide it evenly among seven children,
starve yourself,

with your endless goodbyes
as your children leave for America,
one, two, six, eight, leave,
again and again you wave goodbye,
never to see them again,

with your curses and screams
for Sara, the last one left,
Sara, the atheist, Sara, the Communist,
Sara, you scream, was God's punishment to you,
Sara, the one who sang your praises

for this:
you had only one loaf of bread to feed your family,
and you gave half a loaf
to the beggar woman with a prayer—
if you had to beg, you would be fed.
Your whole life was a prayer.

MALKE

Grandma
in the shtetl
you were Malke
queen
every Passover
you'd get a new dress
and walk
up the main street
people would say
there's Malke
the melamud's daughter
in America
you were called Molly
Molly doesn't mean
anything
in America
your parents sent you
into the factory
a girl sacrificed
for the money
to send your brothers
to school
those educated boys
would never marry
a factory girl like you
you worked hours
in the shop
to send your sons
to college
your sons laughed at you
made you
the joke of America
called you
nasty names
in all their books

you told me
be a good Jewish girl
a good Jewish boy
will marry you
Grandma
in America
your grandsons
married shiksas
an old woman
you sat alone
by the phone
waiting
for your sons to call
your grandsons to call
they were too busy
too busy
making it in America
too busy
making it with the shiksas
too busy
to listen to your stories
they called them
bobimayses
old wives' tales
too busy
to call you by your true name
Grandma
I listened to your stories
about Passover in the shtetl
I listened to your dreams
about school
you could never go to
and socialism
you never lived to see
I knew your love
enveloping me in the kitchen
enveloping me now
after your death
I call you by your true name

not Molly
Malke
in her new dress
on Passover
walking up the main street
Malke
the queen
of the whole world

Malke: in Hebrew the word means "queen"
melamud: a teacher in a religious school

THE SONGS OF TWO SISTERS, HANNAH AND GALIA

If you listen
to the light
to the waves
you can hear
Hannah singing   Galia singing
I lit shabbas candles, went to mikva,
made hallah
I rode the crest of revolutionary Russia,
ran away from home, ran guns, ran presses
I married the Yeshiva boy, had a baby,
had another baby, yet another
I ran to America, rode the waves of strikes
into the streets, the jails
I sang the songs of my grandmother,
of my mother to my children
I sang of the waves that bore me,
one after another
We sang of the light dancing with the waves
If you listen
you can hear
the two songs blending
you can hear
us singing.

My English name, Julia Ann, is the Anglicization of the Jewish name Galia Hannah. Galia in Hebrew means "wave." Hannah is an acronym for the three traditional tasks of Jewish women within the religion, lighting candles for Shabbas (the Sabbath), going to mikva or the ritual baths in order to keep the laws of ritual purity, and making hallah or white bread, and giving the priestly portion of the bread as an offering. Thus the poem is essentially a meditation on my name.

KNOTTED STRING

I. THE PINK STUCCO HOSPITAL

The last time I saw grandmother:
I drove through Reseda,
parked by the pink stucco hospital,
turned right, opened the door.
You sat half-naked on the bed at twilight
in a barren white room.
The dresser had photos of the Family.
The night table was covered with the *Freiheit*.
"It's morning," you said.
"I just got up. Who are you?"
I sank to my knees.
My tears fell on your hand.
You poured rice crispies into two bowls.
Your hand shook.
The rice crispies fell on the floor
and you handed me a bowl.

The *Freiheit*: a Yiddish socialist newspaper. "Freiheit" means freedom.

II. BULBES: THE POTATO SONG

One Friday afternoon in your kitchen
you turned the bowl in the mixing machine.
The machine whirled.
You handed me the bowl dripping
with chocolate batter to lick
and chop, chop, chopped the livers.
We sang, "Zuntig bulbes, montig bulbes, dinstig and mitvoch bulbes."
Sunday we ate potatoes, Monday potatoes, Tuesday and Wednesday
    potatoes, Thursday and Friday, potatoes.
"On Shabbas we had a special treat," you sang.
"Potato pudding," I answered.

Every Shabbas was your family dinner,
the same order of dishes,
the world was right,
fruit salad bowls on each plate,
chopped liver, matza, rye bread in the middle,
you loaded the table with matza ball soup,
chicken, red jello, salad, kugel, meatballs, carrot tzimes,
as if to feed the world,
the last to sit down,
near the kitchen door,
the first to jump up,
tonight, for me, the birthday girl,
you carried in my favorite cake,
chocolate on chocolate.

III. SHIDRIN

Those hot July days in your kitchen
you dealt out a hand of gin rummy
and told me stories,
"When I was a girl in Shidrin.
Shidrin, my shtetl in Russia, the woods.
I ran to the woods.
We met, six children,
and sang to topple over the Czar.
Oh, we sang."
You scooped up the cards,
dealt another hand,
started another Shidrin story.

One day you found me
untying knotted string.
"Yes," you said, "you'll make a good Jewish wife.
So patient. Shaneh madeleh.
I'll make you a shidduch just like in Shidrin."
Shidrin, Shidrin echoed down those years.

At seventeen I tried to escape you by the kitchen door,
"Grandmother, no more stories.
I'm leaving. For college."
"Here," you said. "I never went to school, here,"
a crumpled-up $5 in your hand,
"a gift for college."

Shaneh madeleh: pretty girl
Shidduch: a marriage match

IV. THE TEAKETTLE

"At seventeen I sewed pants in the factory.
Nights I ironed, I mended, I washed
for my five younger brothers and sisters.
I handed my papa all my pay,
got back two pennies a day for the trolley.
Another day. I sewed pants, more pants.
I wanted a penny for a roll. Just one penny.
The union organizer. I signed up.
The first. My union card.
I saved pennies for the grocery store.
Behind the counter of my store. Ten hours. Twelve hours.
Married. Kids. Sliced the rye bread.
Measured out pats of butter. Dished out herring.
Saved pennies for the striking miners in Kentucky.
Nights, upstairs, the tea kettle boiled.
A knock on the door.
A cousin, a landsman, a comrade, come in,
come in, a cup of tea, some strudel.
We sat around the table,
spun dreams of the revolution.
My life,
untying knotted string,
with my union card, my penny bank, my tea kettle on the stove
whistling."

Landsman: a person from the same town in Europe.

UNZERE VUNDERBARE, FARBRENTE MEYDLEKH
(OUR WONDERFUL, FERVENT GIRLS)

I celebrate my grandmothers,
greenhorns, fresh from the shtetl,
dreamers, firebrands, rebels,
who refused to be cheap fodder
for the ravenous garment industry,
refused to be ground up, ground down,
who united by the thousands in a
river of fire that poured into the
Cooper Union strike meeting,
their fire dampened by the union men
cowering at the front table,
who saw red-haired Clara Lemlich
run to the front, one of them,
a Jewish factory girl,
heard her explode into Yiddish,
"A general strike should be declared now,"
who shouted, screamed, stamped,
waved their handkerchiefs into the air,
thrust their arms into the air,
pledged, "If I turn traitor to this cause
may this hand wither from the arm I raise."

Yes, I celebrate my grandmothers
in her own language, Yiddish,
"Unzere vunderbare, farbente meydlekh."

I celebrate my grandmothers,
the twenty thousand strikers of 1909,
who when attacked by mobsters and whores
stood fast on the picket lines,
after their faces ran with blood
still returned to picket the next day,
day after day in the New York City winter
on half a loaf of bread to eat,
went to jail by the hundreds,
scrubbed floors in the workhouses,
sprung from jail they shattered
thousands of years of silence with
fund-raising speeches in
union halls and society drawing rooms,
whose victory inflamed the world.

Yes, I celebrate my grandmothers
in her own language, Yiddish,
"Unzere vunderbare, farbrente meydlekh."

GRANDFATHER

In the family photos he is always the smallest, the short
man from the shtetl with his American son and daughter
half a head taller. When I was a little girl and ate a
piece of meat, my mother told me a story her father told
her when she was a little girl and ate a piece of meat.
"In the shtetl on Shabbas my sister's fiancee came to
dinner. My brothers passed the bread. Chaim passed it to
Yashirya who passed it to Nokum who passed it to Meyer who
passed it to Morris who passed it to Rachmiel who passed it
to me. My mother put the one piece of meat on the fiancee's
plate. A little piece just like your little piece. And we
watched him eat his meat." He repeated, "A little piece
just like your little piece."

THE FLAME

Now let us light the holy candles
and mark the sorrow.
> Morris Rosenfield, 1911
> from his poem on the Triangle fire

I want to cry not pray
this Friday twilight
with the match hovering
above the white Shabbas candle.

I burned
that chilly December morning
when my white flannel nightgown
caught fire from the gas heater.
My back scorched when I pulled
the nightgown over my head.
My singed hair fell out in clumps.
My hands turned yellow and oozed.
I screamed and rocked

just as
the hundreds of girls on the ninth floor
of the Triangle garment shop in 1911
rocked up and down, up and down
on the treadle before they burned
and screamed in the fire.

The flame
on the match still burns.
What did the Rebbe say?
"There is so little joy in this world.
We light the candles
to bring joy into the world."
This Friday I will not cry.
I light the wick
to celebrate the Shabbas.

MY ANGEL TOLD ME

I'm trapped in this moviehouse,
the same film plays endlessly
about Shirley, the girl
from the wrong side of the tracks,
stupid, fat, funny Shirley,
when an angel flew onto my shoulder,
dragged me into the projection booth,
pulled the plug, laughed as she
spread her wings around me
and curled up beside me in the corner.

"I'm Shirley," my angel told me,
"from Lawrence, Massachusetts, 1912,
when the textile mills spat out
women with scalped heads,
tuberculosis corpses,
children with crushed hands.
I stopped the death march
that left the mills nightly
when I opened my paycheck one day,
32¢ short. I'd starve.
'Short pay,' I screamed.
'Short pay. Walk out.'
The whole room exploded,
'Short pay. Walk out.'
I unleashed them,
the Flying Squadrons who ran
from room to room in the mill
yelling, 'Out.'

On strike we were always singing.
25,000 linked arms, snaking
around the mills, singing.
At the strike meetings
we always ended singing.
The women peeling potatoes
at the relief stations were singing.
And after the firemen turned
their hoses on the line we were singing.
And after the policeman clubbed
the pregnant women
and after the militia gunned down
two strikers and after the cavalry
attacked the funeral march
we still took over the streets
in a moving sidewalk linking hands
thirty abreast thousands singing.

We ran out of food
that winter in Massachusetts.
Our children were hungry.
What could we do?
We sent them to other cities.
They were all we had. We sent them away.
When we took the second group
to the train station the militia attacked
the mothers with their children.
That outraged the nation.
That won us the strike.

We always sang in Lawrence
as I sing to you,
remember this your whole life,"
my angel told me
as she spread out her wings,
waved goodbye from the windowsill
and flew away.

I WAS A COMMIE KID

and I hid under the table
terrified when the sirens screamed
for the air raid drill.
The Commies were coming.
The ones I saw on TV.
The FBI always caught them.

We were the Commies.
Grandmother taught me to care
for the poor people of the earth,
taught me that Russia
was my fairyland,
my workers' paradise.
Always, I was the good guy,
I was the bad guy.
The two guys fought it out
inside of me
and I hid for years terrified
if I spoke up
the FBI would get me.
I read in the newspaper once
the offspring of the Communists were vermin
that polluted the country.
Thanks, America.

I tell you my grandmother survived
the ravages of
steerage, the ghetto, the factory
with her loving kindness.
She taught me the truth—
the bad guys are the greedy ones
and the good guys care
for the poor people of the earth.

WHEN I GREW UP

I was the girl who loved
my soldier uncle in Korea.
My best gifts came from the war:
a furry white teddy bear,
blue thongs, a red Japanese doll.
I wanted to marry a soldier
when I grew up.

I was the girl shocked by
the burnt flesh in Vietnam,
marched for years against the war,
saw cops with shotguns on the rooftops,
tear gas rain out of the sky.
Still, I was the girl who believed
they'd never shoot at us.
That afternoon they shot at us
was when I grew up.

WHEN THE CLOCK WAS SMASHED

I.

And I was a plump nineteen,
and I was a green bud gently opening
and I sat with Chili, my first lover,
on the stone bench laughing
with the laughter
rippling through the spring.

II. TIME STRETCHED LIKE A RUBBERBAND
AND SNAPPED

for Diane

Watts abortionist lobby.
Chili and I sat side by side.
Black and white.
Hot July day.
We waited for the doctor.
And waited.
And waited.
And waited.
And the fear
scalded me.
The doctor.
At last.

The doctor stood over me,
screamed at me,
down on the table,
"What's the matter with you?
I have to do a pelvic.
I can't do the pelvic."
My flesh had clenched up.
I've curled up
inside a snail shell.
His words bang at me,
"I can put something inside of you.
You'll abort later.
It might hurt."
I wanted to curl up even smaller
to escape him.
I can't.
He pounded at me,
"Black girls of sixteen don't
give me any problems.
You're twenty.
You're white.
Why are you so afraid?
What's the matter with you?"

I waited in the lobby.
Chili's inside talking to the doctor.
Why is it taking so long?
He's not pregnant.
I wanted to scream,
"Where's Chili.
I want Chili.
I'm not coming back here
for an abortion."

Chili drives back to West L.A. He said,
"The doctor told me not to see white girls."
I wanted to smash my head
against the car's glass window.

III. COLOR JUAREZ WHITE

I was twenty, alone in Juarez, and afraid,
in a white-walled clinic wearing a white paper gown.
The abortionist took from the drawer
his metal rods, metal knife, metal spoon.
I laid back on the hard, white table,
the gas mask was put over my head.
It was over. They wanted me. To stand up. Walk.
I wanted to fall asleep on the floor.
Stood up. Walked. Got into the taxi.
Collapsed against the taxi's back seat.
White street lights. The taxi stopped.
The driver's voice,
"Walk across the street,
and catch another taxi back to El Paso."
At the corner, the other side
looked miles away.
I wanted to fall down.
One foot off the curb.
Both feet.
White headlights.
Cars screeched.
I walked slowly,
step by step.
At the corner
I stood
alone in Juarez.

IV. HEMORRHAGING

"You're OK," the doctor said
in the Beverly Hills office.
Three days later I bled out blood clots.
Pain exploded in my stomach.
I called the doctor.
"I don't remember you," he said.
I was a boat cracking down the middle.
"Take pills," he said.
All day, the pain, the pills.
I was a boat going down, down,
down in a storm.

The next morning I woke up
to waves of pain,
one after another after another.
I drag myself to the phone.
I didn't understand.
The doctor said I was fine.
"Meet me in the hospital," he said.
Chili drove me down the freeway.
I moaned, "My stomach hurts."
At the hospital I'm torn away from him
onto a table where I float adrift
in a sea-white room.
The doctor loomed overhead,
"You're twenty.
We need your parents' consent.
Money down."
Later he told my mother
I was running out of blood.

V. THE HALL OF MIRRORS

Eleven years I have carried that summer on my back
and lived like a cripple, curling in on myself.
I always wanted to take a chalk eraser,
wipe off the whole summer when time stopped,
the clock smashed, the hands wrenched apart.

Down the years I run through
an endless Hall of Mirrors.
I look for Chili, down one tunnel,
up another. I never find him.
All I see in the mirrors
are the doctors.
Blood is on the floor.
My dress is smeared with blood.

SHE'S STILL WAITING

She's waiting for him.
Behind the curtained windows.
Her body's come undone.
All her parts are hidden in folds of the quilt.
The detached hands light another cigarette.
Bring it to her severed head.
The fractured legs walk to the radio.
The toes turn it on.
The legs return to bury themselves in the covers.
The trunk plows deeper into the quilt.
Every time the phone rings it jumps.
She is waiting for him to come.
To hook her head onto her body.
Fasten on her arms.
Screw her legs on tightly.
Wind her up.
Set her out in the world.
He hasn't called yet.
She's still waiting.

FROM YOU I WANT

I see you stone walled in.
Even making love with you
I never touched you.

My father told me
I was stupid,
I was crazy;
the world outside was dangerous.
I've always been
the girl who looks out the window,
hearing the world's roar,
too afraid to go out.
I've always
envied a man's freedom
rather than look at how
I've spun my own chains daily.

All my life
I've been a junkie for sweet words
or a smile.
I wanted tenderness,
not believing it existed,
too afraid to ask,
so I always played the stoic.
So desperate to please,
fearful he might leave,
I would never criticize.
He left anyway.
I don't want this,
anymore.

I want more
than bits and snatches of you, want
a person who does more
than graze the edge of my life.
I want a lover
not encased in stone walls
but one who opens himself
up with archways
beckoning me in.

IT STARTS

wanting you
it starts
between my legs
moves up and out
soaks my flesh
I lie down on my bed
and feel you beside
me like a ghost
your hands haunt me
gliding gently
over my body
aches wanting you
so much
I can hardly bear it

TELL ME ABOUT MEXICO

This morning
I woke up
not angry
at you
in Mexico.
Come back.
Knock on
my door.
We've been
fighting
too long.
No more.
Before
you sit
down I'll
kiss you.
I don't
want to say
anything,
just feel
your legs,
your hips,
your chest
against me.
Tell me
about Mexico
later.

MYSELF UNDIVIDED

You want the parts of me,
the hand that softly ruffles your hair
when you're upset from work,
feet, arms in the kitchen
cooking you dinner,
back, shoulders enclosed within your arms
as you lecture,
breasts you caress in bed;
each part you want, you take,
ignoring the rest.
I insist, there's more,
the parts integrated into a whole.
I insist on myself undivided.

JEWISH MOTHERS

I knew Jewish mothers.
Sara, my great-grandmother,
had eight children gnawing at her.
She was eaten up,
unable to mother her youngest,
a sick baby. She handed it

to Molly, my grandmother,
a little mother at ten years,
who rocked the baby. It lived.
For years Molly mothered
her younger brothers and sisters.
She was sucked dry,

with only screams for Sara,
her daughter of eight years,
"Work in the store." My mother,
an empty shell holding me,
with no breath to breathe into me,
just the words,
"Children eat you up."

I was empty, with
a raging need to be given,
afraid if I had a baby
I'd be so poor I'd claw the walls.

THE MOTHER TAKES HER DAUGHTER

The mother takes her daughter
in her arms,
the daughter who waited for her first dance
to start in her white high heels;
her pendant hung from her neck,
a microscope etched in gold
she won the previous day—
the best science student.
She ached to be asked
when the boys picked the girls
to escort into the hall.
Alone she walked in
at the end of the line,
fighting the tears.

The mother takes her daughter
in her arms,
the daughter who cracked the instruments
in chemistry class
and smiled at the boy next to her,
"Help me, please."
He puffed up,
and asked her for a date.
She wanted to smash
her head against the wall;
her brains would splatter apart.
She'd hand them
on a platter to her date.

The mother takes her daughter
in her arms
and comforts her.

DONNA'S POEM

You only remember
that girl in faded cotton.
She withered under the looks
"poor white trash."
She sat in the classroom,
bit her tongue
not to blurt out "ain'ts."

You only remember
that terrified college girl
in homemade shirtwaist, afraid
she was an impostor,
the mask would crumble,
the looks of scorn again.

You forget the dreams.
When you were a girl
you would soar
above the clouds.

THE GIRL FROM THE SHTETL

I want to give not only that which I am, but that
which I might be if only I had the chance.

—Anzia Yezierska

The girl from the shtetl was silent for millenia,
only the man sang,
the man sang a marriage song to the girl,
only the parents sang,
the parents sang a marriage song to the girl,
until the twentieth century uproar arrived
when the girl started to sing,
     a song about wanting to see life,
     a song about wanting to go to school,
     a song about wanting to go to America,
     das Goldene Medina, the Golden Land,
No one listened. She hung herself.
When her parents cut her down
she was still alive, still singing.

At my family dinner table
Mama, Papa, Aunt, Uncle, all sang the same song,
     Cousin Larry is going to Law School.
     Cousin Barbie has her second baby.
I wasn't a singer but a dancer
like my cousin Rose
whom no one ever sang about.
In hushed tones Mama once said,
     Rose was a modern dancer.
     That was bad enough.
     She married a Black and
     no one ever spoke to her again.
I stopped dancing and wanted to die.

Anzia Yezierska—the first Eastern European Jewish woman to become a pro-
fessional writer in the United States.

Instead I ran away,
ran away to the land of words,
the words of poems, novels, plays,
after I lost the dance,
I wanted the words,
the words that came out of the golden land,
the words were torturous to get out,
if I send them out
the Family will do to me
what they did to Rose.
For years I fought my terror.
Each word took me closer to her fate.
One day I wrote, Dear Family,
        What ever happened to Cousin Rose?
Mama wrote back,
        Rose teaches dance in New York City.
So I wrote to Rose,
she wrote back,
        the girl from the shtetl
        came to America,
        became a union organizer,
        rented me my first room
        when I was alone in the city,
        keep writing, keep writing,
and now I, I make words,
I send them out into the world,
these are my words,
my Goldene Medina.

I WANT TO SAY THE WORDS

Every morning I wake up crying
I was butchered in an abortion.
I make up speeches to myself,
if a part of myself gets killed,
let it die.
I can't stop crying.

During the abortion I always said,
it didn't hurt.
I wasn't afraid.
I stood up, walked ten paces, sat down.
I said, "I'm fine."
I stood up again, walked three steps
and wanted to collapse on the floor.
"I'm OK," I said.

All I've ever wanted
when the memories come back,
when I start to shake,
is for someone to hold me.
"Please don't bother yourself," I said.
"I'm fine."

Dying was fascinating.
You wind down slower and slower;
when you're dead
you've wound down completely.
When I start to remember
I can never ask for help.
What if the answer was "No"?
I'd splatter apart.

I give up too easily.
I have kept safe within my shell
so no one will notice
how much I hurt.
I have hung on to it
too long;
the only way to let it go
is finally say the words,
"Just hold me."

REQUIEM: FOR ROSAURA JIMENEZ

Alive she was a graceful eagle,
determined to escape from the ground
where her parents, farm workers, stooped down,
she spread her wings to fly to the sun,
college, plans to be a teacher,
so intent on that distant sun, a diploma,
she never spent her scholarship for a
legal abortion, chose a cheap hack,
abortion cutbacks removed her safety net,
that hack shot this eagle down,
in the hospital she kept on falling,
her trachea was cut out,
blood spilled from her eyes,
and only then, wings broken,
body crushed, did she plead to die,
an eagle crashing into the ground.

Rosaura Jimenez was the first woman to die after Congress cut off legal assistance to poor women to get abortions.

IT'S NEW ORLEANS JAZZ

Jennie the wino
sure can play
that beat-up piano
in the LA Skid Row
soup kitchen,
all of her plays, yes,
all two hundred pounds,
not minding the men
at the coffee urn
or the white toast tray,
when she's sober
she only plays gospel
now she's drunk
it's New Orleans jazz
and Jennie sings
the blues

THIS ROSH HA SHONA

I've been learning new words
all this week you've been in the hospital—
malignant, bone scan, liver scan;
cancer has its own vocabulary, its own time:
tests were on Monday; results, Friday.

I miss your green eyes,
curly black head,
poking through the doorway
of my office with jokes.
The months you went from one doctor
to another you still
poked your head in with jokes.

I miss your hand on my shoulder,
your words that helped me,
new on the job.

I even miss your worrying.
Oy, you worried,
about the spaceship falling to earth,
the Vietnamese boat people, Israel.

This Friday on Rosh ha Shona
I will come to see you
with apples and honey.
May your New Year be as sweet.

FOR A HITCHHIKER

41

Sweetheart, I gave you a ride,
the woman drowning in the wet streets,
with your stringy black hair,
your straw basket full of clothes,
drank in all of your words of
your rape, your lost daughter,
drove you around for hours
until I found a crash pad for you,
left you by the old Victorian,
a home for you. I said I'd return.
Three hours later I was back with
a knapsack, blankets, food stamps.
You were gone, they said, gone.
I hope you live through the night.

KADDISH: FOR ANNE FRANK

I. THE HORNS

Dear Mr. Frank,
Sometimes in my dreams I see Anne (and) I wake up
screaming before my dream ends.
                    American Jewish girl, fifteen

My parents never spoke of the Holocaust.
When I read Anne Frank's diary as a child
she was the first Jewish girl I read about.
She had brown hair and brown eyes like me.
She loved books like me.
She was the only one for me.
When I watched the movie,
I cried waiting for the end,
for the Gestapo horns to screech
through the dark night streets of Amsterdam.
My parents never spoke of the Holocaust.
They always said "the war."
"Mrs. Novak had trouble at childbirth
because of the war."
When I was twenty-eight after a Friday dinner
my father finally told me about our cousins in France.
"In 1939 they wrote asking me to help them
come to America. I never wrote back.
I had no money, no friends in high places.
What could I do?"

II. THE FOOTSTEPS DOWN THE STAIRS

For years I've been obsessed with Anne,
with knowing what happened after the diary closed.

To begin: How was Anne arrested?
Not at night but on an August morning,
the sun danced with the water in the canals,
Anne at the kitchen table dreamed of school,
that summer after D day she had rejoiced,
wrote down every Allied conquest in her diary.

The Gestapo walked quietly up the stairs,
opened the door softly.
You stood up, waited silently.
The Gestapo sergeant looked so ordinary,
chunky, the face of a gas meter reader.
"Jewish trash," he said, "a big haul, eight of them."
He ripped open your briefcase,
your diary, your papers
fell like sad angels to the floor.

Already you disappear from me.
Now, to save myself, I must follow
your light footsteps down the stairs.

III. AND YOU WERE HAPPY

At Westerbork, the Dutch concentration camp,
the Jews stand in groups of five in the big square,
five Jews, five Jews, five Jews. The Nazis gave
the Jews wooden shoes in the wrong sizes.
Anne has a new name, "convict Jew," new clothes,
blue overalls, a red bib, new wooden shoes.

You were a caged animal for two years,
hiding behind dusty windows, dirty net curtains,
aching for the outside. Now at Westerbork
you walk home each night from the workshops
holding hands with Peter, your sweetheart.
Always you two walk round and round Westerbork
—two candles which light up Europe.

IV. LOOK, LOOK

We soon came to the end of tears.
We scarcely saw and heard any more.
But Anne had no such protection to the last.
                    Mrs. de Wiek, on life at Auschwitz

Where is Anne, for 55 days at Auschwitz?
Block 29, Mrs. de Wiek screamed, "I'm thirsty,"
stuck out her tongue to catch the rain,
so thirsty she thought she was going to die.
Anne somewhere begged a cup of coffee, returned
to the barracks to hand Mrs. de Wiek the cup.
Hold this moment. I've had enough.

A bird attracted by the smell of Auschwitz
I am forever flying above it, the dead breath
of the world below on my neck.
There's only one way to go, down,
to follow Anne around for 55 days.
Her head was shaven, her hair packed pipe joints,
her face thinned, her eyes grew bigger,
two black pools reflecting the stars.
She marched with her group past the Jewish children,
the children at the door of the gas chamber.
They waited all day in the rain for their turn.
The other women turned their heads away.
Anne said, "Look, look," and she cried.

V. THE GRASS THAT GROWS AT BERGEN-BELSEN

Anne was sent to Bergen-Belsen
into the heart of the black sun.
The blackness eats her up.
She is lost to me there.

I can not go to Bergen-Belsen,
I can not go,
I can not,
I've been fleeing for years
but the road always circles back,
I must go to Bergen-Belsen
to help the Jews.
This time
I walk down the road lined with death's heads,
hear the wind howling across the empty moor,
go into the camp
to trail behind the typhus
as it cuts through the prisoners like a scythe;
I catch them and ease their fall.
Still no Anne, all I see
is hunger easing into every human pore.
I will fly the world,
collect packages of food,
bring them back to Bergen-Belsen.
There, one of Anne's friends.
I throw her a bag.
Now I see the faint outlines of Anne,
a shadow, a wraith, crossed by barbed wire,
screaming for food.
My Anne, what they have done to you.
Watch,
your friend throws you a bundle across the wire,
sugar, zwieback, a tin of sardines.
Your white hands thrust against the night.
Anne, I will send you more.
Hold on. The Allies are coming in one month.
They came too late.

I hate the grass that grows at Bergen-Belsen,
hate the pine trees, hate the moss.
I would burn it all, then
lay myself down on the scorched earth and cry.

VI. SIX CANDLES

And Yom ha Shoa, day of remembering,
I put on a black arm band,
walked into an auditorium full of Jews remembering
two thousand Germans walked for Anne Frank
from Hamburg to Bergen-Belsen
on her death-day remembering,
and on April 19th I remembered,
a girl over her schoolbooks is sacred,
a girl walking with her sweetheart is sacred,
a cup of coffee is sacred,
sugar, zwieback, a tin of sardines are sacred,
as I watched the six survivors at the front table
light the candles,
one for each million,
one, two, three, four, five, six.

Two books provided the historical documentation for this poem:

For Anne Frank's history after her arrest,
Ernst Schnabel, *Anne Frank: A Portrait in Courage*,
New York: Harcourt, Brace and World, Inc. 1958.

For the impact of Anne Frank's diary,
Anna G. Steenmeijer, ed. *A Tribute to Anne Frank*,
Garden City, New York: Doubleday & Company, Inc., 1971.

Part I.
Letter of fifteen-year-old American Jewish girl to Otto Frank, from *A Tribute to Anne Frank*.

Part IV.
Statement by Mrs. de Wiek from *Anne Frank: A Portrait in Courage*.

BLAZING STAR

Once I rode the crest of the wave
of change that swept the world until
the shotguns blasted us,
my friends bled on the pavement,
the movement "we" fractured into "I's,"
the decade died
and I was cocooned in numb despair.

I emerged from my cocoon to see
the empire we live in crumple
another million lives in the colonies
where the torture racks kept turning,
the napalm kept falling,
the death squads kept shooting so
we in the Capital could cruise
the cafes in the latest fashions.

I saw the sacred rites of my youth sold
as status symbols. People bought them,
even to putting designers' names on their jeans,
wanting to pose, ass out,
wanting to climb up the ladder of success,
not speaking to the people on the rung below
to teach them their place.
What land had I lost myself in?

I had forgotten
how once I rode the crest of the wave.
If some people want to stand still,
let them.
I want to be moving again—
a blazing star across the night.

ODE TO WOMEN POETS:
NERUDA REWRITTEN

I salute
the ancient light flying
out of the earth.
The endless
thread connecting
women and poetry,
this long
silk thread
has never been cut.
It runs
as far back
as human memory.
It saw with her eyes
tumultuous spring
being born,
the baby's first step,
the first kiss,
and in wartime
she sang of peace.
There was my Greek sister,
blood on her head,
with her lyre, singing
among the dead.
She was called
Sappho,
Muriel Rukeyser.
Her lullabies
then and now
were a white flight,
a dove,
were peace,
an olive branch
and beauty's continuity.
Later

she took to the streets,
the fields,
I met her singing
among the cornstalks,
celebrating
love affairs
between women and men,
between women,
between men,
telling of the pains
in childbirth,
recounting
the sweatshop girls'
death by fire
or the ghastly nights
of rape.
They, women,
blues singers,
poor among the poor,
sustained
on the strength of their songs
the human smile,
they told of the millwomen's
misery
and the Hindu widow's
implacable fate.
They, women
with a battered harp,
and eyes that knew
life,
carried a rose
in their poems
and showed it in the backstreets.
Women,
you are
the keepers,
the weavers
of poetry,
humbly proud

across history,
the surge for liberty
and backlash,
across the sun and the moon,
the earth and the stars.
And now
the treasure
is here in my country,
English lilacs,
the LA Santa Ana,
the blues that
surmount calamity,
the hand of sisterhood
on the road,
the word
repeated in song
from mother to daughter
and passed on,
the wind's rhapsody,
the voice that needs
no bookstores,
everything we
have to learn
from her truth
our song's eternity.

In this poem I have rewritten an English translation by Stephen Kesler of Pablo
Neruda s "Ode to Popular Poets."

UNDER THE LADDER TO HEAVEN

That bitch, the angel
weighed on my back. She
                    warbled
"Sacrifice. For others.
You don't deserve. Not you."

For years
that green and white beauty
                          sang.
I yelled "Shut up" in vain.

It's too damn much—I
jerked, threw her to the ground. Up

she jumped; back I pushed, up and back
we wrestled for days
                  until

I submitted. She was off guard,
relaxed. I grabbed her,
swung her
            round and round.

With all my force
              I threw her
into the sky; she circled above, screeching.
                            I threw rocks

at her. She flew up, up to
disappear.
And with a shout
              I began
to climb the ladder to heaven.